Reflections in a Mirage

Reflections in a Mirage

AN ANTHOLOGY OF POETRY

Gurkeerat S. Randhawa

PARTRIDGE

A Penguin Random House Company

ISBN: Softcover   978-1-4828-4808-3
               eBook   978-1-4828-4807-6

Print information available on the last page.

To order additional copies of this book, contact
Partridge India
000 800 10062 62
orders.india@partridgepublishing.com

www.partridgepublishing.com/india

Contents

Part III
Desperate Defiance

Part IV
Last Vestiges of Dreams

Part V
A Surreal Rebirth

Part VI
The World Beyond

Part VII
The Odyssey of the Soul

Foreword

Gurkeerat is a young, aspiring poet, driven by a strong yearning for poetic self-expression. He seems to have convinced himself that words alone matter, and that he must fashion a poetic world out of his creative longings. *Reflections in a Mirage* is his first ever publication, and apparently, he is quite excited about the fact that it would launch him into the world of letters. On reading this collection, one finds it hard to believe that this is either the first work of a struggling poet or it is the work of an amateur poet, still struggling to find words for his emotions, ideas and experiences.

Reflections in the Mirage deals with a range of themes such as invocations of childhood, youth v/s old age, mortality or transience of life and some ponderous reflections on such philosophical questions as "search for light", "uncertainties of life" or "insignificance of human existence". Interestingly, these are the ideas that have intrigued and fascinated poets down the ages. In his treatment of these themes, Gurkeerat sometimes displays a child-like naiveté and sometimes, bubbling effervescence of youth and sometimes, profundity of a man, wiser much beyond his years. Gurkeerat uses a large variety of forms such as rhyming couplets, free verse, haiku et al to create his poetic universe.

The present collection has been divided into seven sections, though it is not quite clear why Gurkeerat felt the need to do so. These sections are neither theme-based nor do they project any kind of linear progression. Perhaps, they only betray a sense of circularity of ideas and themes, which, in effect, becomes a hallmark of his poetic flourishes, too. In the first section, the opening poem titled *The Bird of Hope* captures the attention of the reader instantly. Its special appeal lies in the directness of expression and highly nuanced, striking imagery. "To the bird, all the lines and limits/ Of mankind are blurred/To him, all nations, all people are one/No barriers stand between him and freedom."

Coming from a young adolescent, still on the threshold of youth, these lines are quite remarkable, and display a definite degree of maturity of thought and expression. Gurkeerat is a sensitive young poet, gifted with an overpowering imagination and broad-ranging sympathies. When he looks around at the world, nothing seems to escape his poetic observation, and whatever does finally fall within the purview of his poetic expression, is dealt with rare spontaneity and even remarkable sincerity. Sensitivity of this young poet can easily be judged from the way he captures such cadences of thought as: "They stare back at moments that seem like years" or the way he mourns "the loss of the sunflower."

Occasionally, one is startled by Gurkeerat's unexpected moments of epiphany, his momentary flashes, and his sudden discovery of truth or abrupt recognition. At one point, he literally throws you off-balance when he says: "life is on the other side of the bubble," and at another by suggesting that "I am but a drop in the vast ocean." In one of his poems, he compares himself to a traveller "who is amidst the darkness of all uncertainties" and therefore, is "in search of light." Sometimes, Gurkeerat also slips into a kind of prosaic turgidity, especially when he is unable to match up to the constraints of rhyme and rhythm. *The Visionary* and *The Prism of Ambition* are two such poems where his struggle with words almost shows and the concreteness of expression gives way to certain nebulousness, even vagueness.

Fortunately, this is something that happens only very rarely, that too, when Gurkeerat is struggling most apparently with the words as well as the constraints of rhyme. Most of his poems lack amateurishness, and are an absolute delight to read, especially if they are enjoyed in a desultory, somewhat lazy sort of a way. Among the poems I enjoyed reading the most, some of my personal favourites are: *The Return to Life, The Phantom of the Desert, The Gardener's Loss, The Shadow of Flame* and *World Exposure.* There are many precious gems and pearls that lie scattered in these poems, only if one is willing to dig somewhat deeper. Then one is certainly rewarded with such astounding lines as "For tomorrow, I may not be the same anymore" or "Where contentment is all man needs/Where contentment is all man leaves behind" or "My world is a desert of thoughts/where the only oasis of solace is death."

Despite all its good qualities, I recommend this book to the reader with a definite word of caution; that s/he must approach it somewhat indulgently, with the knowledge that the poet is a young adolescent and also a first timer. One must not don a mask of seriousness and start judging these poems in one's characteristic, stentorian manner. The reader must flow with the current, step into Gurkeerat's poetic world gently, and then slowly immerse herself into his experiences, with as much sympathy as he has shown while dealing with his subjects. These poems do command the attention of all kinds of readers, and I'm sure, shall be enjoyed equally by a cross-section of readers.

I congratulate the young, upcoming poet Gurkeerat, and wish him all the very best for the success of his maiden venture. I sincerely hope that he would continue his affair with the written word, in one form or the other, and move from this success to much greater success.

Rana Nayar
Professor
Department of English & Cultural Studies
Panjab University
Chandigarh

Preface

"Genuine poetry can communicate before it is understood." -T.S. Eliot

Dear Reader,

Life is quite a strange matter. Yet, it must be the strangest in the younger years, in the silent black forest, shrouded in the mist of uncertainty, veiling the horizon of tomorrow. Unfortunately, I'm still passing through this very forest, so I can't say much else about the world, except for that which I see here. It is still quite a wonder, for while the pains of frustration and the joys of discovery cloud my thoughts, I feel like a change arising in me each day, transforming me into another person, one who I will be for many decades to come. In these moments, I look back at my steps, at the path I have taken, wondering how it brought me here and where it will take me now. Even today, my mind remains perplexed by this very question, though unable to provide the answer that I seek, it puts forth a strange thing to me in its lieu--Poetry.

These verses are thus, in essence, efforts of my soul to demystify my own familiar yet alien existence; this book is therefore, not just an anthology of poems, but a repository of answers. Hopefully, you may find some stark and clear answers of your own amidst this struggle of mine. This is precisely why I believe that this collection and the poems therein, have ended up being neither too simplistic nor too erudite, but somewhat indifferent: An outcome that can only be justified due to them mirroring the very world they try to portray. Although, beneath this mundane shallow surface, there exists in them a ray of hope, of light emerging from darkness, soulfulness out of indifference, just as it does out there in the world. For even if you stare down the darkest abyss, you will believe it has some end to it. That is how we conceive infinity, that is how life and death are simply conceptions to us. I have written these poems upon the precipice of change in my life. In the end, I have but looked into that abyss and written down my conceptions.

Even though those conceptions may be mine, I firmly believe that this work wouldn't have been possible, had it not been for the constant support and encouragement of my loved ones. I'd like to thank my parents and elder brother wholeheartedly, for if it weren't for them and my other close friends and family, this work's inception would have been nearly impossible. I also express gratitude to my beloved school, an excellent institution that has always provided and continues to provide me with an education of the highest caliber. I'm truly blessed to be among such a plethora of caring and open-minded people every day, I owe my art to them.

On my part, I can humbly say that I've strived for the best I could with these poems. I've tried putting on paper the sheer profundity of human emotions; the truth behind the myriad minor happenings that together comprise our lives; the inspiration that drives all of humanity to reach out and achieve its highest ideals and dreams, not just every now and then, but every single day, by every single person; alas, the sublime beauty that makes life truly worth living. I have tried and I know that I'm not the first to do so and that I won't be the last. In spite of all of this, I sincerely hope that these mere words on paper will reach out to you, beyond the passage of daily life, and remind you yet again of an often forgotten truth: Life is beautiful.

Gurkeerat S. Randhawa

Part I—The Advent of Hope

The Bird of Hope

There is one bird that glides upon the edge

Of this garden of life every day,

He soars among the wind and above the clouds

Settled high in the bounds of the sky.

Whenever a man's eyes turn upward,

He floats away in endless beauty

That inspires the hearts and souls

Of the many that are bound to land.

Often he looks down upon the surface

Seeing people go on with their lives,

Their days marked with struggle,

Their years marked with uncertainty.

To the bird, all the lines and limits

Of mankind are blurred,

To him all nations, all people are one,

No barriers stand between him and freedom.

To that one bird, all men are also free,

To that one bird, the world is valuable,

To that one bird, everything is perfect,

To that one bird, life is beautiful.

At its heart, the true spirit of humanity wishes

That whenever men would look skyward,

They would not only admire the beauty of the bird

But also, if only just for a moment, believe in what he believes.

The Visionary

All people say that they already have what they truly want,

And that no more remains for them to earn or attain,

That from now on, not more light, but only darkness it is

Lying ahead: The difference of those who can and can't.

Even here, life goes on by the power of differing thought,

There, where others find death, one finds a brighter life,

There, where others find limits, one finds an endless extent,

And by this, the world to this one day was brought,

Not the first such day, nor will it be the last,

Such goes on the life of men, and of the world itself,

With change years can't count, mountains none can mount,

Where the near future is simply to be a renewed past.

For there is a vision, an ambition, a dream to pursue,

That drives a man to do so or not, to be forever or never,

To reach out into darkness, never settle for anything less,

To find a brighter life, and make his dearest dreams come true:

"Rise up, rise up, above and beyond this earthen sphere,

For what a heart as true as yours shall ever seek

May only in illusion here lie, or in delicate dreams to die,

You will ultimately attain something farther and higher than here."

The Prism of Ambition

O, the Earth and the Sky
Remain distinct to my eye
Only since one is where I am today
And to the other I mark my way.

It is but through this one prism
That I see the world, for which we endeavour,
And though the end may lie beyond my sight,
I live only to pursue it forever.

The prism of a man's ambitions
May be narrow or may be broad,
May be shallow or may be profound,
A visionary leader or artists seeking applaud.

Whatever be my prism of ambition,
Through which I see the world, the transient visage,
All my hopeful acts will go on till the end,
Yet one may last a lifetime, another many an age.

In soaring hearts, and rising spirits

There lies the universal spark of life, beyond strife,

The burning desire that culminates into legacy,

The ambition that spends our great life.

O, for the Earth and the Sky

Remain distinct to my eye

Only since one is where I am today

And to the other I mark my way.

A Day Prayer

Oh great one, today may I learn to embrace and love

All my brothers and sisters as I may

Never have before; to be one and united

With them in the union of your everlasting

Equality and impartiality.

In the essence

Of my deeds, my thoughts and my relations

May there lie the subtle stroke of your

Divinity, in the truest form of love

And affection for all and everyone.

May I learn to surpass all the illusions

Of differences and needless longings and desires

That may seem to overpower the truth in

My day today, and live beyond them.

Alas, grant me the courage and the

Power by which I may only follow the ideals

Of that which I believe the most: If I choose

Not to be selfless, forgive me, but I promise

To remain true to myself; if I choose to

Remain arrogant in times of humility, forgive

Me, but I promise to remain true to myself.

But dear God, I finally wish that though

I promise to remain true and honest to myself today

May the truth in my deeds, thoughts and relations

Ascend to much greater and far more superior

Heights by your magnificence in times to come

That I may lie peaceful and tranquil in the

Subtlety of my mind, the wielder of truth and wisdom,

And that I may be ever-present and ready with endless

Power and will in the vigour of my body, the wielder of

Power and force, and in the gifted balance and beauty

Of both these may there be the union of life

Bound together by me, to be lived wholeheartedly by me.

So that in my day today may there be nothing that

May prove difficult or impossible for me, and that in my

Success and attainment may I prosper and fulfill all I can,

Whilst uplifted by you and your great world,

That you have let me live in for so long and so well.

Beyond Today

How will the river flow on to the sea if there remains no water
within it anymore?

No tide will ever be formed, great or small,

If there is no coming shore.

Alas, how will life go on

If here I let the river run dry before the ocean comes,

If here I let a shore arrive before a tide may ever arise?

And how will this man's life go on

If, in times of despair and tragedy, his spirit

Cannot murmur to him one final time:

"Everything will go on, and so will you, my dear friend,

All rivers, all tides have but only the same end.

And upon each passing way, only remember the truth that

Moments different from this will still one day come, beyond
today.

This present, howsoever rich or poor, shall ultimately change
and grow into

The future, which you can make as bright as you want,

A future which you can live just as you want,

For the everlasting opportunity of happiness, and peace,

And life yet is there for you, beyond today... beyond today."

Redemption in Liberty

Go on, my friend, go on

Through this world to which you are bound-

This body, this heart, this mind, this soul

Behold within the truth of what you are,

The truth of what you want to be.

Just for this moment, forgo and forget

All the chaos, the struggle, the illusion around,

And set yourself solely in one direction

To the destination which neither fades nor comes again,

The one every man has yearned and still yearns for –

Freedom.

Let yourself reach there, let yourself be free

Not by being yet another passing shadow lost in time,

But by being apart, by having been,

By having lived, and by yet living in a world,

Where your life is what you want it to be.

The Moment

A great man it was once

Who, long ago, told me of life,

Of a life of true humanity,

Of just being another one

That knows the truth yet can never speak it,

That knows of death yet can never face it,

That knows of a threshold yet can never cross it,

That knows of life yet can never live it,

And ahead all of this he still comes to live a moment

Further in life where he will laugh, and smile,

And be happy, and live to such depth and truth,

That all this will not matter anymore, only life will.

For life goes on beyond all this... at this very moment.

Part II—Desires Despite the Call of Duty

Life-The Midst

To have merged with such a life,

That ever changes like the seasons of time,

Not in blossoming, not in withering

Is a flower's beauty, and its truth,

Not in the beginning, not the ending

Lies the brilliance of the tale,

Not in the sunrise, nor the sunset

Shines the bright day.

And that, as all these,

The wonder of all things is, alas,

Not how they came to be, or how they

Shall fade, but in how they are,

In how they shall remain here onwards,

For that is what counts - The Present - for only

The true depth of life shall last on, and all else,

Even these powerful emotions are but only momentary.

We shall yet go on, and within us shall

Go on life, without any regard, endlessly.

For not in the starting, not in the end

Is the good, the true, but it is in the

Midst of all else, within us, as us,

Living on whatever there may ever be,

Living on for evermore, as the great

Is everlasting, beyond all else, despite all else.

Thus I shall go on to live in the present,

And that no shallow change, or suffering, or anything,

Can separate me from who I am, from what is,

For all has now long begun, and before all shall now end,

Just as any great thing, I shall now make the middle such

That this flower shall bloom forever; that this tale

Shall go on forever; that this day shall shine forever;

That when this ends, may it be worthy of once having been.

The Midnight Artist

I live in art, in each moment I find

The deep truth of myself, which otherwise

I would forget in my passing days.

Alas, then the beauty of art strikes me-

That I, too, am a human being,

And that I am but as everybody else around me,

And how a moment of mine could mean a lifetime to them,

As they could and have always done the same.

So, here I hope to leave the marks of artistic legacy,

A promise by which I shall forever stand,

That beyond this moment ages may pass,

Though this shall remain the same piece of work

Of my devotion, my art, my humanity,

To all people who may come and go past this

One place where I leave a part of me

To complete their lives, if it shall, whosoever it may be.

Gurkeerat S. Randhawa

The Gardener's Loss

Each day the shadows of life pass over me,

Where I can do no more than reach out with my hand

In a human effort to catch those I please

And let go off me those which seem to follow me

As my despair. I strive for the afar with only hope,

Hope nothing more than a mere thought of mine,

And that is it, my means of life end here.

With these only I must live and nothing more.

The rest are all the same, of the fragile and momentary kind,

Like a delicate vase that thinks itself to be something else

Altogether, simply because it has pretty flowers in it.

But when these flowers shall forever wither and fade, and

When the vase is needed no more, what will become of it?

Today, one such vase's scattered fragments lay in front of me

Upon the back window, in a form that seems irreplaceable,

And impossible to be revived by some more flowers.

But I can do no more than look back

At this moment as just a moment of sorrow,

But for what reason do I cry?

Do I cry for the fallen petals which were once a

Beautiful flower; do I cry for the many pieces of a once

Delicate and memorable vase or do I only cry for

The selfish reason that both the vase and the flower

Have left my house, my garden for evermore?

If so, then I shall go on to cry for this sorry gardener,

This man whose garden's essence has now gone such that

No season, no love, nothing can ever bring it back.

For ultimately, though life will go on, as it always does,

I cry for my truest loss... for my loss of humanity.

The Shadow of Flame

I walk further each day

Towards the ultimate end,

Where my flame will fade to shadow,

And till then there will come a day

When I choose to shine so brightly that

When alas darkness falls upon me, still

A glimpse of my light may live on as the

The true flame of all others, and let these

Young shadows of flame, one day, become

The very flame, the light themselves.

World Exposure

How long can I go on with this bubble-like existence of mine?

Delicate as can be, something that survives by only a thin thread

Poorly drawn out by me only for a while longer now,

A part of the world, yet closed off from its truth,

Not just because I choose to be ignorant in my fear of the world,

But because there is no other way for me, or for anybody, if we are

To live as has been intended by all of humanity, as is hoped
by us.

Alas, even this one event is only a momentary one,

And upon the day that this bubble shall eventually burst

I can only imagine how immediately I would suffocate in this
alien world.

It is either that day, when the world will descend upon me

In all its brutality and harshness when I am oblivious of it,

Or this day, today, when I may prepare for the coming storm

That awaits me as much as I possibly can.

So that when ultimately this bubble of mine may burst,

May I be the least bit ready to survive all this, and live beyond it.

And if not that alone, may I come to know the truth of this world
    and of me,

Which is yet only on the other side of this safe and warm bubble.

And I embark upon this adventure today, not knowing if I shall
    return

As what I was, or if I shall ever return at all from this experience,

This exposure, this world, this truth, this newfound life of mine.

A Limitless Threshold

What divinity is there to whom we pray

And grant our praise?-I yet truly can't say,

For as all things that exist and live,

And reap and sow, or cease or give,

I, too, I am but insignificant and uncertain,

But of me long after having gone, remnants will remain,

Be it legacy or only remembrance, just as all great things

I pursue and hope to be, and there is a way to give my ambition
wings--

I live and I am, therefore I can rise or fall. Either way,

I come to know of this-That there is a reason to why we are here
today,

Why alas we have come to live in this world, and why in it we
are more awake than asleep,

We have a choice but to make ourselves insignificant, as all have
deemed, or to have an impact deep

Upon this surface of everlasting existence, where life has forever
dawned and grown,

And amongst it I only aim to be nothing besides respected, loved and known.

For ultimately, as all, to the divinity I pray, and hope for what my life may come to be,

I strive to rise and succeed, this is my choice within, and this is the life I live, the only world that I see.

The Railway Station

Deep within the urban extents

Of the mighty metropolis,

Stands the old establishment

Where people across the country

Flock together to travel,

Through cramped compartments

Where the scent of poverty and suffering

Ever-lingers, as strongly as it does on the station.

The stench left behind by those who have drained

The tracks and walls in their waste

Is only met by those who pass by,

As they can merely express disgust

For the endless filth that they see,

The dusky faces of the locals and travellers

Bear distinct black-and-white eyes

That stare back for moments that seem like years.

Each minute that a brown old train arrives

Desperate porters leap to the arriving travellers

To carry their heavy loads so that they may earn a living,

As the well-to-do men, women and children

Walk along without a care in the world

Amidst the endless struggle around them,

While from some lonesome corner comes

A herd of hopeless beggars into the crowd.

One person stands among all this, within all this

Just standing there, perhaps waiting

Either for a train or to leave the station,

Happy that he is leaving it either way,

Although in the long meantime

His heart melts for a crying infant,

Or a crawling leper, or maybe just for himself

As he envies his many peers at the station

Solely because they may have a better thing or two.

Soon, a stumbling train or relative arrives to get him,

To get him far away from the railway station

Where he has spent some of the most eventful,

Most sickening, most revealing, most human,

Yet the most unique moments of his life,

Then when he has finally reached his seat in the train

Or the parked car of his relative,

In a flash of a single moment, as long as any other, he leaves, he is gone

Like just another gust of wind of the many more to come and go.

Forgotten Days

The fields of my childhood,

I still remember them today.

And I would cross them dearly every day,

As an innocent and ever-ready child,

Oblivious of his surroundings, but deeply glad

Of all that he saw, even where the skies were grey,

Or the blossoms faded, he would go around happily,

Truly believing that it's a sunny spring day.

A child not held back by his own self,

There were no limits to his imagination,

And certainly none to his lively doings.

But when this grown man remembers him today,

He may just laugh or smile at the innocent person he was,

But he may never come to know, within his bound self,

That this child was far freer, truer, and happier each day

Than he may ever get to be, or at least feel to be, in a lifetime.

And he may still not know that, despite whatever the world
may say,

It is always possible to return to that beautiful childhood,

Such that when it may rain, instead of hiding away,

He may reach out and drink the sweet rainwater

That when he may fail or suffer loss, may he know

That all things will come and go, but this one smile that he retains on

His face right now is what truly makes his life in this world valuable.

Yet whatever it may be, he will always remain that child within,

But maybe just not for now.

A Single Sunflower

I was once lost in the visions and dreams

Of a far-off horizon that never fades,

My spirit was but only pursuing endlessly

The great light of life among these dark shades.

What I could have ever done and been

Back in the freedom of the measureless past

Now is not true anymore to my mind and heart,

For along with time, a shadow upon my heart was cast.

Till this day that shadow eclipses

All my golden hopes, which barely can now pass

Through the still threshold that now changes everything,

And sadly my hopes no more remain golden, nor do my dreams
  remain alive.

Like a once bright sunflower,

That looked up evermore to the great sun,

And followed beauty, and freedom, and happiness,

Only up until the storm had come,

In the endless fields where all sunflowers once laid,

In the hopes to surpass all, aspiring to grow farther,

There's now only barren land and colours of life, none,

While a single insignificant sunflower withers away

Recounting the glory of the past, that shall never return.

Though one day the storm will move on.

But, flower has already gone, leaving behind only

Fallen petals and a broken stem, just simply there,

Lying lifeless, devoid of the chance of truly living anymore,

And so they remain no more, struck by everlasting loss,

The young sunflower remains no more.

A Side Within Me

A side, a spirit, a being,

Why does this yet here live on?

Is this only a shadow that I am seeing,

Or is this truly something still not gone?

And as dawn does finally in the dark creep,

As all tides do alas fall upon the shore,

So does this spirit awake within us deep

To take us farther than this, for evermore.

For in the end, say we all that we may,

Whether words of lasting or of fading,

Beyond all else yet lies the truer day

Where not the sea, but the river is forever flowing.

Just as all things must pass on to be

Either great or mere and less or a lot,

So then only one side shall it be of me

That shall ultimately tell what I am or not.

That side is me and otherwise is all but nothing,

It may in my brightest day ever hide,

But above all else, it is surely something

With which my visceral self shall forever abide.

And, of all things that shall go on,

This side is something else, something far higher,

For this is my shore; this is my dawn,

This is who I truly am; this is the pinnacle of the spire.

Part III—Desperate Defiance

In Search of Light

Oh, the days and nights pass by,

They go on for me as they do for the many others,

All those who live the life of worldly endeavour,

I am but a drop in that vast ocean

Of the multitude of men, women and children,

Though still a drop I am, though still significant,

Even if there are a million others like me within this ocean.

I am but yet another one struggling to do my best,

Although along this momentary road of endeavour

There runs the river of life besides us all,

Running the currents of constancy,

The winds of endlessness, the light of beauty.

We all may follow this road of ours till the end,

But the river besides shall go on forever, beyond our horizons.

As yet another traveller of the road,

In the midst of my efforts devoted to humanity,

My sight strays to the ever-shining and glorious river,

For be it the day's bright sun or the night's full moon,

The sheer glow of the river never ceases to be.

A stumbling traveller like me often finds inspiration

And rises up to his road simply by this one captivating sight.

Within each traveller's worldly self

I believe there is an innate spirit, a true soul

Which, though ever-ambitious upon the road,

Longs for but one drop of water from the river,

For one drop that may enthral, may mesmerise, may uplift one

To thresholds of magnificence and amazement such

That I believe they are what makes existence truly worthwhile.

I am but like those travellers,

Like one who amidst fulfilling his worldly destiny

Seeks a momentary refuge, a sanctuary,

Like one who amidst the ways and ends of his endeavour

Seeks an impermanent haven, a trance,

Like one who amidst the darkness of all uncertainty

Seeks one precious little beam of light, a beautiful thing.

Like one who is in search of light.

Transient Passion

Whenever my heart is overcome

With emptiness, devoid of passion,

Impatient, unfulfilled, hollow,

I wonder how the generations of men

Before me endured this fleeting agony,

And then, my heart finds serenity,

Consolation in the fact that eventually,

All of us go through the same times,

It is only our view of the world that

Transforms our lives, and that is all.

Promise of a Revolutionary

Rise, oh my brothers, rise up today

For it is only change that can give way

To a greater and brighter tomorrow

When our transient joys may leave,

Yet, my brothers, our spirits shall forever heave.

How Freedom Moulds a Man

Upon a bright and pleasant day

A youth did in an orchard lay,

Not soon, he chased a radiant red apple falling

When, at once, he heard the calling

Of an elderly man far away,

Saying, "Son, let that apple fall where it may."

And the youth had let the apple fall its way.

Down came the precious apple and scattered and broke

Like a soft red rose harmed by human stroke,

The enraged youth simply stopped and stood,

Regretting what he had done, and thinking what he should,

And he knew that only acting upon his own belief,

To stand out alone for himself, like a drop of dew on a leaf,

Will ever in this world do him any good.

The youth now tall and independent stands

And aspires to go farther, beyond these lands.

The Fool in Love

When someone asks me what truly is love,

I then do only speechless remain,

For what I truly behold within, is far above

What any mere words may ever succeed to explain,

But if it were to come to then saying so,

What makes love so special, so great,

I would only then say that it makes one grow

Into something else, as it further opens life's gate,

And when you enter within, past that gate, that door

Which all life your either never cared to see,

Or could never pass through, it enlivens you for evermore

And then life is the truest, the brightest thing to ever be.

But alas, I believe that it is love's sheer beauty and simplicity,

Like a single bloom in garden, insignificant it may be though,

Shall stand out to this mortal eye, as a life spent well and greatly

In true and lasting love, where these sweet words forever flow:

"O dear Darling, we did in our sweet lives

Experience something beyond all other things to be,

For which every being in this great world strives

So that they may go on to live with one, complete and happy."

The Eternal Lover

Tell me, would you mourn if these very eyes of mine today,

Tomorrow were to become but only shadows within death's abyss,

And be lost in darkness, unable to see you, unable to feel you

And your everlasting presence? Everlasting not for my eyes but somewhere

Else within forever, impenetrable and forbidden to all others, even this death,

But except you-For there forever my spirit stands guard, for there forever

My love for you, for everybody, for the world, for life stands guard.

And I love and embrace you today, for I know it is all of me that

Will last, it is all of me that will yet bind me to my whole, that is you,

And still let me live on, in none else but the light of true love, when all else fades

Into countless fragments of many earlier forms, when all else dies, and I suffer the same.

But I shall never die within this heart of mine that shall last on,

Remaining ever-still and stable, when all else around me, of me, with me,

Shall collapse into the very abyss where I too shall lie, ever-enlivened

With your love, oh my dear.

For whatever may happen to this mere form of mine, no matter how many

Fragments it shall break into and separate, no matter how it shall fade and die,

Within me you still will remain, within me life will still remain, but alas

Only to love and to embrace you just once more, for evermore.

The Candle of Life

Oh my dear soul, my friend,

You have walked me through life

Ever since the day it all began,

And still do always,

Upon many a day and night

You have played with this candle

That I hold in my hands,

Many times you have breathed to it

To brighten its flame,

And many times you have held your palm

Around it, to hide its light,

Anytime that you have ever done so

It has been for my good

In this world, so that I may live well,

But each and every day, sometime

At moments often beyond daily passage,

I look upon this burning candle

Longing for freedom, for life,

And however we may treat this candle,

It burns on, but I believe it is not pain and suffering

That prolongs, but a wish, a hope that lives on,

So for once, my friend,

Let's not make this candle small or great,

Let not life run by some needless method and way

Which does not let this candle burn as bright as it truly can,

For once, let the candle burn bright when it shall,

And alas let it fade when it shall, let life be free from now

On and for once be only a sweet and true part of a beautiful
world.

Gurkeerat S. Randhawa

Wandering Youth

I wander through the endless lands,

Lost in the spirit of myself, in my thought

And yet also lost in the world that I see.

I am overcome by the passing fields

Adorned by the million people and lives that pass by,

And feel as though I am forever a part of it all.

And as I see these million little parts

That together form my entire world,

I am awe-inspired by this truth.

For one moment of time,

All my daily ways and feelings fade

And give way to something else altogether,

A feeling of a great oneness with everything,

Though I may never even come close to describing it,

I have but only one word for this feeling - Fulfilling.

The Phantom of the Desert

O, lost deep in the endless dunes

That hide the bright orange horizon for me,

When all I can see is dreary dullness, I sigh in despair,

For my world is a desert of my thoughts,

Not much growth of true and distinct purpose exists,

And I am lost in the transient desert of my thoughts,

Where the only oasis of solace is death.

Till that oasis shall come, ahead of these dunes,

With the rivers of blood and sweat that I shed,

I hope to provide the channels for my pipe dreams,

And as my own dunes of stature and success may grow,

My strength, my purity and my truth is lost.

So, I strive to become a phantom

Who hears and dances only to one melody in the world--

The melody of mere earthly achievement,

The dark and dull phantom that lives and dies,

Gurkeerat S. Randhawa

Having forgone the beautiful essence of life,

The phantom whose enjoyment and happiness in life

Is as non-existent as truth and goodness in his soul.

In a time long ago, all I ever wanted was to see

Just for once, the colours of the horizon beyond the dunes,

But now, at their very pinnacle,

All my heart wants is the form of simplicity,

The transience of destiny, and the lustre of truth

Of the sands beneath, which forever

Blow on with beauty upon the winds of the horizon.

Though ever-engulfed in the anonymity of time and space,

The real world lives in that bright sand, not upon dunes

At that humble level of existence, the shapeless grains

Of sand ascend higher in a few precious moments in time,

Than the impermanent dunes of phantoms ever will.

The Beggar

Day-to-day upon the ever grey street

He, like homeless wind, wanders around,

But alongside him there lays only the fleet

Of countless equal ill-fates to none but sorrow bound,

And some few laugh, while the others cry,

When within they are only the same man,

But alas when all these & other thoughts pass them by,

To far-away, hopeless extents their minds are ran,

But their woes are not yet any wounds deep & true,

That the world of all the others of better fate and kind

Are regardless to them for evermore, when these few

Have been defeated in the world, but never in their mind.

If through these endless storms they can endure,

And despite such poverty yet such wealth possess,

If in these cruel contaminations they can remain pure,

Then they, as all else, to the world shall be no less,

But he, the beggar, only in a humble wish desires

Not for more content to blot out his true heart, like us,

But for the harsh winter only small and warm fires,

He desires only what is needed, and forever remains thus.

Then if such he can at all times remain,

That he may learn to live beyond what we call wealth,

Is he not worthy to leave behind this ceaseless pain,

This plague of happiness, this ailment of health?

The world lives on among its supposed joy,

Its supposed health, its supposed fortune & satisfaction,

Yet still it does elsewhere such true ability of life destroy,

Does there its highness, its greatness recede from action?

For in the end, there is no difference, simply nothing

For him, the beggar; for him there is no ambition to win;

For him there is no longer the hope, the capacity of anything

Besides what the world has reduced him to, as finally he cries within:

"May at once then come on end that fateful day,

When wealthy and poor, high and low may all equal lie,

That if not in life, then at least in passing away

A man may content and peaceful die."

Part IV—Last Vestiges of Dreams

A Return to Life

Whenever my heart was lost in time,

And my mind was resting in surreal peace,

Whenever the world would ever relieve me

Of all that I live, and live for,

For some reason, for some will of mine,

I would prefer that my peaceful rest may go on,

But yet more I would desire a return to the world

Due to the endless struggle and suffering of which,

Nevertheless, I go on to be, I go on to truly live.

And so now I return to my sweet home,

To fill the void within me... with life.

Gurkeerat S. Randhawa

The Apple Garden

In some different season of time,

Among all that consists of my world,

I stand in an orchard, just like any other,

Looking around quietly, lost deep in my actions,

But I find around me only the fallen apples

Which whenever I pick up to eat are either dry or rotten.

Hopelessly, I still go on, searching for at least

One last good bite for the day.

My day of hunger goes on and on,

Along with time, and as it passes,

I wear down, devoid of hope,

I lie in despair upon the ground, in the worthless garden,

Saying nothing, doing nothing, thinking nothing,

Just waiting to forget my failure,

And besides me there lies one last apple,

Which I believe I have not seen or tasted,

And I pick it up in my final effort, I bite the last apple

And just as I can bear no more, a ripe freshness

Flows into my mouth like pure water from a perennial river,

And lasts till the end of my day.

I truly realise there at that moment, that I would

Never have given the single ripe apple the respect, the value

That I did, had it not been for a hundred rotten ones,

And ever since I eat both the kind with wholehearted joy,

Knowing that one would only lead to another sometime,

And that in the end, I would have spent a day to remember.

Regretful Laziness

Laziness often does become a part of me,

A void of darkness amongst all the other

Great qualities that I may have,

Destroying even the very best of me.

Each day I wake up, hoping to

Finish some forgotten, undone deeds,

For talent and skill may only serve a purpose

In life, if they are used day-after-day in sincere work.

And each day has now long passed away.

The Flower Petal

Once there was a time,

When I was the very essence of a flower

That towered above all,

With its beauty and glory.

And out about me

I saw the world,

And all its wonders and joys,

And all its suffering and sorrows.

But the endless vision

Of the earth and the sky

Enchanted me, bringing me

Closer to the horizon far away.

And soon it happened

What I truly desired,

When a storm arose and changed everything,

A new beginning disguised as the final ending.

In my despair at that moment,

I never knew why all of it was happening,

And instead of reveling in the thought of change

And my fulfillment, I only cried in the momentary mourn.

When alas I was falling,

And my earlier home had gone,

When the flower, my entire world,

Was destroyed, and when there was a deep void within me,

I felt only pain and despair,

And thought that life itself would now cease.

But a falling petal like me went on,

Falling into unknown darkness.

Finally I reached the end

Of a single passing hour of life,

And found comfort and peace

Where I never would have thought,

The earth, the soil which all my life

I looked down upon, not knowing

That it is from there only that I sprung up

And came in this world, and today I reunite with it,

Rejoining with my true whole after years above,

And now though I might be devoid of a source of life,

As a single petal like me cannot go on by itself,

I feel born to a second life, a second world.

The wind now blows me where it wishes,

And passes me on far and far away

From there where my entire world was based,

Away into a quiet corner in the forest.

Where though I might spend my last few moments,

I believe I have lived a complete life,

Not in all those years before, but today, for one day

I have lived such, that I do not regret leaving.

And I find peace and happiness,

And fulfillment and joy, where I lie right now,

Believing that never will I live another such moment,

And that in itself makes my life in this world worthy and true.

The Sunlit Valley

Far away from the ever-sweet home

Where I would weep and laugh equally

At all times, here in darkened ways,

Where I can do no more than only be disheartened,

I stand, down in a corner where the perilous world

Spares me a small bit of sunlight, but only some,

I stand, upon the brink of collapsing,

Yet I continue to remain upright and willful

Knowing that my life is worthy of each and every last effort.

For I shiver in the cold dark today,

So that tomorrow I may, even if only a little bit,

Value the bright sunlight, which I receive

In those precious moments of life I often let pass and forget,

And just know within me somehow, somewhere

That I would be willing to live on in anyway, if it were to lead

Me to and let me remain in this everlasting warmth of sunlight,

And that I would never let any of it go, ever,

That I would strive to live a worthy and valuable life in this world.

The Last Remembrance

Don't be sorry yet, oh true heart,

Not now when these incomplete things

Might seem to be your complete life,

For in the true entirety of life,

It is not these mistakes and errors that count,

Nor these singular successes and momentary rises,

And at this moment, I am merely whispering a small

Syllable of one minor word among the great lexicon of life,

By it alone I cannot measure all else.

It will all go on, moment-after-moment, year-after-year,

And when all these moments that, for now, seem ultimate

Come to an end, and when they are all eventually together,

Being the substance that was once my life,

I believe I will find something far more significant than all this.

Something immeasurable, and at that final moment of remembrance in life,

When it is the truest, I will only look back upon it quietly, peacefully, maybe even happily.

When the Tide of Change Sweeps a Man

I can only try not to forgo an opportunity

That I believe will come again tomorrow,

For tomorrow all may not be the same anymore,

For tomorrow I may not be the same anymore.

The Twilight Spirit

Whenever dark nights of despair overcome me,

When the bright sun of the sky is nowhere to be seen,

When the hope of the heart and the might of the mind

Shall only fade into the dust, of what had once been

The very essence, the very life of me, and never again will be.

Then only one thought is borne by me:

Of how the greatest tragedy of every man in this night

Is the everlasting truth that he will always find

That he believes darkness overpowers light,

That despair overcomes happiness--Alas, that this is to be.

To Those Who Are Close To Me

Oh my dear companion of life,

Within this ordinary outlook,

Beneath this seemingly scarred surface,

Is a unique and sincere soul,

Which I shall remain to be.

The Enduring Spirit

The passage of a spirit

From age to age

Marked with the essence of time,

Of all that passes on

And comes to this one day

When one true heart

Shall be lost in the mist

Of a single moment when

Peril and fear would overshadow all,

And the once strong heart

Now shattered and faded

Lays lifeless among the dust,

Having not known long ago,

What all life it has lived

And still shall, if only in this... it ever believed.

Part V—A Surreal Rebirth

The Soaring Spirit

Oh, whenever the wings of my soul

Soar upwards to the sky,

Whenever I am uplifted, and

Transcended to greater heights,

Lost in fleeting moments

Passing by like the wind,

Yet flowing endlessly,

To breathe life into all things.

It is only then,

That ever do I realise

Just how small I truly am,

As I see my loved ones,

My entire life, my daily universe

Lost in some far off corner

Of the world that I now see,

The great world that is my home.

These awe-inspiring moments may soon end,

These beautiful things may someday pass,

But, nevertheless, the one that sees them now

Returns a changed man, unlike all the others -

One that lives and dies, having known the truth

Of how majestic the world is,

Of how magnificent life is,

Of how valuable he truly is.

Lost in Beauty

I once saw a sight that mesmerized many hearts,

Its composition was subtle and strange,

Yet it bore the deepest impact upon me,

For at first, it was lifeless for me

While everybody else admired it endlessly,

And days passed, and years, and time went on

Till finally would come a single moment of life

When my spirit upon looking at that one sight,

After long ages, would finally realise its truth,

And there on my spirit did soar... oh, so great

Beyond all thresholds of imagination,

Into the realm of the everlasting, the beautiful.

And even today in my heart

That one sight, as a world, still lasts.

One Drop of Dew

I stand alone, like one drop of dew

Sliding down quietly upon the bright green hue

Of levitating leaves, having known serenity true,

I go on alone, like one drop of dew.

Ebb and Tide

All that we can do in the world's course,

With its endless currents of peril upon us,

Is but hold onto to the great banks of our soul

That we believe will lead us throughout

To a happy and worthwhile life and then a peaceful end,

Where contentment is all that a man needs;

Where contentment is all a man leaves behind.

The Essence

Oh brother, reach out your hand,
For there is beauty beyond this land,

Far away the horizon you may see
A dimension of life that we all let be,

For the world is not confined
To the bounds of the human mind,

For even beyond imagination and words, there lies
If only a single moment of real life for you,
Adorned with a purpose in our existence true,
It will live on in your heart till the end of your days.

The Pacific Prayer

O, my land is lost in the dearth

Of brotherhood, of humanity,

For as far as the eye can see

There is but blood spilt upon the red earth.

O, the hearts of many do cry and plead

'Where else shall blood be spilt,

Where else shall we all fight and bleed

And let the beauty of life forever wilt?'

If only there was peace for one moment,

Insignificant, yet priceless it would be,

O, maybe true hope will overcome my brothers and me,

And let us end and forget our perennial lament.

Will this be, or will it not,

My brothers, I can't yet or ever say,

But I shall ever utter these words, which humanity long forgot,

No matter how useless they may be, until that great day.

An Imperfect Haiku on Beauty

Beauty lies in the eyes

Of the beholder,

But even those eyes

Take a lifetime to

Achieve perfection.

Part VI—The World Beyond

The Night of the World

The day I opened my eyes,

I was filled with innocence,

Oblivious of this world that I now behold,

Oblivious of what side of it I would live to see.

Then when I grew further,

I learnt about this life,

And how we all must strive

Amongst our very own brothers and sisters,

Only to live on and to make our mark in this world.

As insignificant and short-sighted life seemed here,

I still listened to those fools, some were wise, but I suppose

After all this... life, it was difficult to derive the lies

From the truth, the right from the wrong, it was as if

I was destroying my own true self to improve the ways of the
    world.

But alas, here I am today,

Aged and weak, meek and old,

After having lived life, oh this precious life,

Something that may never come again, and after

Having lived it, I find myself only but waiting for

Its final end to come, the certain end for all.

For I realise, as I wait for the last moment

That all along this life there were many

Answers that I sought, many roads I chose to

Walk, now it seems as if neither those answers

Nor those destinations might ever be felt, might ever

Be lived by me, for evermore.

Is this life, is this it, and is this the end of it?

I might ask everything now, but ultimately my end

Shall be the same as any other person's, but I only

Hope that I had felt all this... this truth earlier,

And that I would have actually lived when I had the great chance.

Alas, I must now leave this world, despite all,

Against all, I must. All those moments I ever

Lived, whatever they were, now seem as distant dreams

Yet to come true, as all things were when I was just

A child, but I believe the time has passed now, it has

Flown constantly like the wind, otherwise without

Its everlasting passing, life for all else would be impossible.

Now nearing this end, I think of everything,

Of life, the world, all, but deep within this

Thought there is still a person, whose life has

Now passed, but whose feeling is no different from

That of all else, regardless, careless, yet only human,

Not knowing that each moment of sadness is each

Moment without happiness, and though some of us might

Say it, but only a few may ever feel the sheer truth

Of such things, of life altogether.

And finally all things start to disappear, all begins to

Fade, and what was once light is now only darkness,

What was once life, now is nothing, and what was once

Me, now may be nothing more than some remains which,

Too, shall perish. This is the cost of life that I am losing each

Moment and this is life itself that I am losing each moment.

At the end of all these years, only one thing seems true to me-

Life, the truest gift of all, forgotten by me, only to never return

To the only thing which ever mattered, but all things must

Come to an end, all that is significant at the end of all things

Is not how great, how strong, how good, or what we were, but

Only what we made of it. And if we were ever, even for just a
moment,

Truly content, peaceful and happy in this time we were given,

If we truly ever lived life in this world we were given.

The Remnant

Along the passage of time,

Ever-going upon the endless road,

There seems only one thing to me

Worthy of my life and devotion.

For this very road all others shall

Pass, regardless, whatever it may be,

And among those countless people,

I, as all else, shall too alas fade,

And that in the end only my difference,

My remnant of life will ever last,

When all else of me shall only become a shadow of the past.

Thus I live such, that whenever I or anybody shall

Look back upon the distance I've come,

The life that I have lived, or yet shall,

To them and to me, it is these memories,

And this very individual that was once me

Which shall brighten up their face,

As they shall finally say:

"Even today, he goes on to be,

If not merely outside, then at least within,

For here he still is, lying beside,

With eyes now seemingly shut, but truly open wide.

For he still, upon his sight and feeling,

Can ever make us laugh or cry,

In the end, to us he is as all emotions,

As all feelings-For he is there, true and near,

Beyond what we earlier felt or thought of him,

Lying formless, yet so powerful and empowering,

And still he lasts, even when all else may say otherwise... still he lasts."

The Being

There is one thought that lies in me forever:

That among all else, I am just another soul,

Amidst struggle, suffering and joy, to form my whole,

In a world where so long lives on each of these, lives on human endeavour.

For Our Forefathers

Oh Mighty one, I pray in silence today

For the sake of the martyrs that sacrificed their lives

For my freedom and existence in this world,

The ancestors, the forefathers of humanity,

Due to whom I stand here today, possessing the gift of life.

Oh, in this tranquil moment I remember

Their struggle of survival and triumph

To which they dedicated their lives,

Just so that me and my brothers of the present,

Their descendants may live as happy and free men.

Oh Great One, bless the souls

Of my forefathers, whoever they may have been,

For to them I owe my life.

Bless their souls so that they may,

Just for a moment, relive the truth and beauty

Of the world for which they lost and suffered in ages bygone.

So that they may know that they lived and died

For the generations of Mankind that live on in hope and freedom,

For the beautiful continuity of life.

Let them remember, Oh God, the Earth of Life.

The Meadow and the Cottage

Along the orange threshold of horizon,

I walk on,

Across the never-ending fields,

I walk on...

Afar there lay one little dwelling,

Which to the eyes of a traveller

Is the remembrance of a former life

Lost in the forgotten wilderness.

Within I enter, within the cottage I enter,

The silent house where many spend a lifetime.

It is the home of only one old lady,

Who comes towards me as I enter.

Her home almost seems a part

Of a peaceful and tranquil nature,

Yet within her brown, little house there is

Just one little clock, the last remnant of the outside world.

Just as the clock, depicting the time,

In vain, going on slowly and quietly,

So walks the old lady,

So lives the old lady.

An integral part of the beautiful mosaic

That lies outside, and even within,

She lives as though her years are pent up

In some sort of stagnant gloom and sadness.

But when my innocent heart

Pondering upon all of this

Ever asks her of her life,

She smiles, as does a joyous child,

She recounts her many

Years of glory, of happiness,

Of love, of success,

Of adventure, of beauty, of life.

She does so with a tone

And feeling of joy such,

That I only hope I shall be so

Happy and content in my own old age.

Alas, she tells me,

That although she confines her spirit of life

Within the cottage in the meadow today,

In times gone by, she truly danced and lived in the meadow.

I ultimately depart from her house, her cottage,

As I resume my great journey further,

My soul now rises and soars,

Willful and ignited with the desire of a wholesome life.

And along the orange threshold of horizon,

I walk on,

Across the never-ending fields,

I walk on...

Part VII—The Odyssey of the Soul

All Shall Pass

Dust disappears, shadows fade
And so does all that they ever made,
The brightest green turns to a wilting grey
To mark the end of yet another day,

And all that is shall one day be gone,
For in the end, life must go on,
What lies here today will tomorrow surpass
The Earth-bound life, for all shall pass.

An Old Friend

A traveller was coming to the end

Of his long and eventful journey,

Down by a bright stream, he saw an old friend,

As the day was passing beautifully,

He stood still and silent,

His gaze upon the other side was fixed,

In curiosity, he further went,

And spoke the words of a man transfixed:

"Oh, before I shall upon this road

Any further go on to ado,

I will relieve myself of Life's load

And be lost in the essence of you."

The old friend didn't speak,

Nor did he ever move from stillness.

The man from then on did solely seek

The quiet haven that would spell-bind and bless.

That day his existence felt like rebirth,

As he was struck down by fate's sharp knife

And he lies silent upon the Earth,

Until the wind shall stir his soul back to life.

The Thought of Lasting

I behold within myself now

The wonder of life,

And if it was granted as it came,

I shall one day relinquish

This magnificent wonder

To those younger spirits,

For whom and within whom

I shall live on for evermore.

Forgotten Legacy

Endless days and ceaseless nights
Mark the lives of many, every day,
Times when some ascend to soaring heights
While the others still upon the Earth lie.

In time, each moment will be forgotten,
Each memory remembered, each marvel cherished,
The once-ripe apples shall one day be rotten,
Ages from now, even our dust would have perished.

Although what we do in life might have an extent,
Until a man's work might still seem undone,
But true legacy is never born in an instant,
Nor does it ever go to die in one.

The Tears of Time

The glorious moments are all that remain

Of a man's long-forgotten memories,

The shattered cage is all that is left

Of a free bird no longer in sight,

Oh, the endless tears of time

Will ever-roll down the cheek of Earth,

Clinging to the surface of the base of life

Being realized by many of us to be the truth.

When the years of deeds will fade

And legacy will be the last performer

Of the symphony of existence,

Mesmerising the multitudes with an echoing melody.

Oh, the tangible and the mere of today

Will ascend higher with each passing stroke

Of time upon its beautiful face

Till when it shall become the cosmic light,

The light that all will look up to,

As the tears of time will descend,

Embodied in us, our souls shall come

And go, bathed in those tears of time,

Oh, as these breaths of life will inspire one,

Lost in the visions of a fading horizon

To prolong in the glory and remembrance that will

Illuminate the world of many more to come and go.

When alas, one tear of our own shall drop

Upon the barren lands of timelessness,

And there shall rest one little seed of our significance,

Which years from now will grow as it will

And be the sole symbol of hope and beauty,

Ever-bathing in the tears of time to brighten the horizon.

The End

Printed in the United States
By Bookmasters